YOU CAN TEACH YOURSELF®
BLUES GUITAR

By Mike Christiansen

D1244347

---

*CD Contents

1 Music Intro (:34)	30 ㉘ (:46)	59 ㉸ (:45)
2 Narration Introduction (2:43)	31 ㉙ (:44)	60 ㉹ (:41)
3 ① (:40)	32 ㉚ (:49)	61 ㉺ (:24)
4 ② (:46)	33 ㉛ & ㉜ (:28)	62 ㉻ (:57)
5 ③ (:25)	34 ㉝ & ㉞ (:27)	63 ㉼ (:25)
6 Strum Patterns 1-6 (1:32)	35 ㉟ & ㊱ (:27)	64 ㉽ (:43)
7 ④ (:48)	36 ㊲ & ㊳ (:30)	65 ㉾ (:38)
8 ⑤ (:43)	37 ㊴ & ㊵ (:30)	66 ㉿ (:35)
9 ⑥ (1:09)	38 ㊶ & ㊷ (:25)	67 ㋀ (:19)
10 ⑦ (:52)	39 ㊸ & ㊹ (:30)	68 ㋁ (:48)
11 ⑧ (:44)	40 ㊺ & ㊻ (:29)	69 ㋂ (:41)
12 ⑧ with Swing/Shuffle Rhythm (:40)	41 ㊼ & ㊽ (:30)	70 ㋃ (:40)
13 ⑨ (:14)	42 ㊾ & ㊿ (:29)	71 ㋄ & ㋅ (:31)
14 ⑩ ⑪ ⑫ (1.05)	43 ㋕ & ㋖ (:40)	72 ㋇ & ㋈ (:19)
15 ⑬ (:40)	44 ㋗ (:49)	73 ㋉ & ㋐ (:19)
16 ⑭ (:32)	45 ㋘ (:51)	74 ㋑ & ㋒ (:20)
17 ⑮ (:32)	46 ㋙ (:45)	75 ㋓ & ㋔ (:18)
18 ⑯ (:43)	47 ㋚ (:47)	76 ㋕ & ㋖ (:18)
19 ⑰ (:43)	48 ㋛ (:52)	77 ㋗ & ㋘ (:18)
20 ⑱ (:37)	49 ㋜ (:22)	78 ㋙ & ㋚ (:21)
21 ⑲ (:39)	50 ㋝ (:44)	79 ㋛ & ㋜ (:24)
22 ⑳ (:49)	51 ㋞ (:24)	80 ㋟ (:40)
23 ㉑ (:45)	52 ㋟ (:41)	81 ⑩⓪ (:39)
24 ㉒ (:47)	53 ㋠ (:25)	82 ⑩① (:40)
25 ㉓ (:47)	54 ㋡ (:47)	83 ⑩② (:40)
26 ㉔ (1:01)	55 ㋢ (:52)	84 ⑩③ (:54)
27 ㉕ (:45)	56 ㋣ (:25)	85 ⑩④ (1:13)
28 ㉖ (:43)	57 ㋤ (:39)	86 ⑩⑤ (:31)
29 ㉗ (:45)	58 ㋥ (:23)	

*This book is available as a book only or as a
book/compact disc configuration.

A video of the music in this book is now available. The publisher strongly recommends the use of thisvideo along with the text to insure accuracy of interpretation and ease in learning.

1 2 3 4 5 6 7 8 9 0

Visit us on the Web at http://www.melbay.com — E-mail us at email@melbay.com

Contents

Introduction 3

How To Read The Music 3

Tablature 4

Strum Bars 4

Time Values 5

The Blues Progression 7

Basic Chords 8

Power Chords 12

Movable Power Chords 17

Barre Chords 21

The Tie 26

Hammer-On 27

Pull-Off 28

The Slide 29

The Bend 31

Vibrato 32

Turnarounds 34

Fill-Ins 44

The Blues Scale 46

Using The Capo 62

Double Stops 62

Common Blues Licks 67

Bass Line Accompaniments 71

Building A Blues Solo 73

Fingerpicking Blues Solos 76

Introduction

The blues is a style of music which was born in America and has become very popular and has influenced music the world over. This style of music is at the very roots of jazz and rock n' roll. Many of the techniques used by the earliest blues players are popular and still used today not only in playing the blues, but in playing pop, rock, and jazz styles, as well. This book will give you the tools necessary for playing blues guitar. You will learn the blues progression, strum patterns, how to accompany a blues song, power chords, the blues scale, how to build an improvised solo, and how to play fingerpicking blues solos. The topics which are covered in this book can be divided into two basic groups: *accompaniment* and *solo* playing. Although the book progresses smoothly from front to back, you may want to skip from section to section depending on what your interest may be. For example, after learning some basic strum patterns, you may want to skip to the section on the blues scale and learn to improvise a basic single-string solo. Then, go back and learn power chords and how to use them for the accompaniment.

The information which is given to you in this book should provide a "springboard" for you to go on and create your own accompaniments and solos. Don't be afraid to experiment. Try creating your own blues songs. If you practice and learn the "tools" given to you in this book, you'll be playing blues like a pro.

How To Read The Music

The exercises and solos in this book are written using diagrams, standard notation, and tablature.

The chords and scales in this book are shown with diagrams such as the ones drawn below. They are pictures of the guitar neck. In the diagrams, the vertical lines represent the strings with the first string being on the right. The horizontal lines represent the frets. The dots show where to place left-hand fingers. The numbers on or next to the dots show which left-hand finger to use. With the chords, the loop under the diagram shows how many strings are to be strummed.

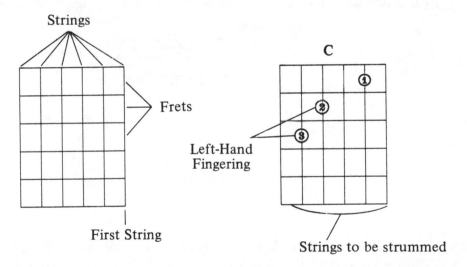

In the standard notation, a circled number next to a note indicates on which string that note is to be played. Other numbers indicate left-hand fingerings.

fingering: 3   1   3   1   3

Tablature

Another way of writing guitar music is called *tablature*. The six horizontal lines represent the strings on your guitar. The top line is the first string.

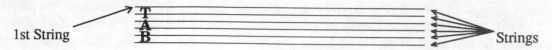

1st String — T A B — Strings

A number on a line indicates in which fret to place a left-hand finger. A stem connected to the number shows that note gets one beat.

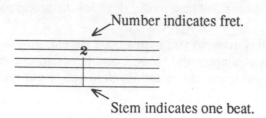

Number indicates fret.

2

Stem indicates one beat.

In the example below, the finger would be placed on the first string in the third fret.

1st String
3rd Fret

3

If two or more numbers are written on top of one another, play the strings at the same time.

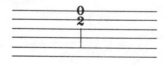

0
2

Strum Bars

This mark ⌠ is called a *strum bar*. It means to strum a chord one time, and it gets one beat. The direction of the strum is written above the strum bar. This sign ⊓ means to use a downstroke. This sign V means to use an upstroke.

Two strum bars connected with a beam ⊔ means that there are two strums in one beat (usually strummed down–up). The chord that is to be strummed is written above the measure.

Time Values

Written below are the different time values of the notes used in this book. The tablature equivalent is written below the standard notation. These time values apply if the bottom number of the time signature is a 4. If the bottom number of the time signature is an 8 rather than a 4, all of the time values are doubled.

	NAME	TIME VALUE

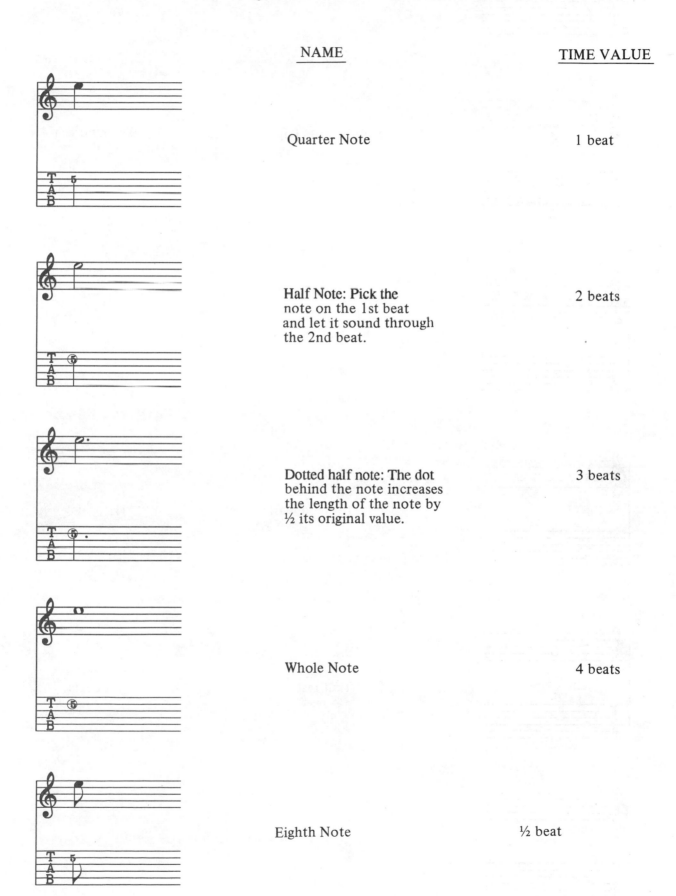

NAME	TIME VALUE
Quarter Note	1 beat
Half Note: Pick the note on the 1st beat and let it sound through the 2nd beat.	2 beats
Dotted half note: The dot behind the note increases the length of the note by ½ its original value.	3 beats
Whole Note	4 beats
Eighth Note	½ beat

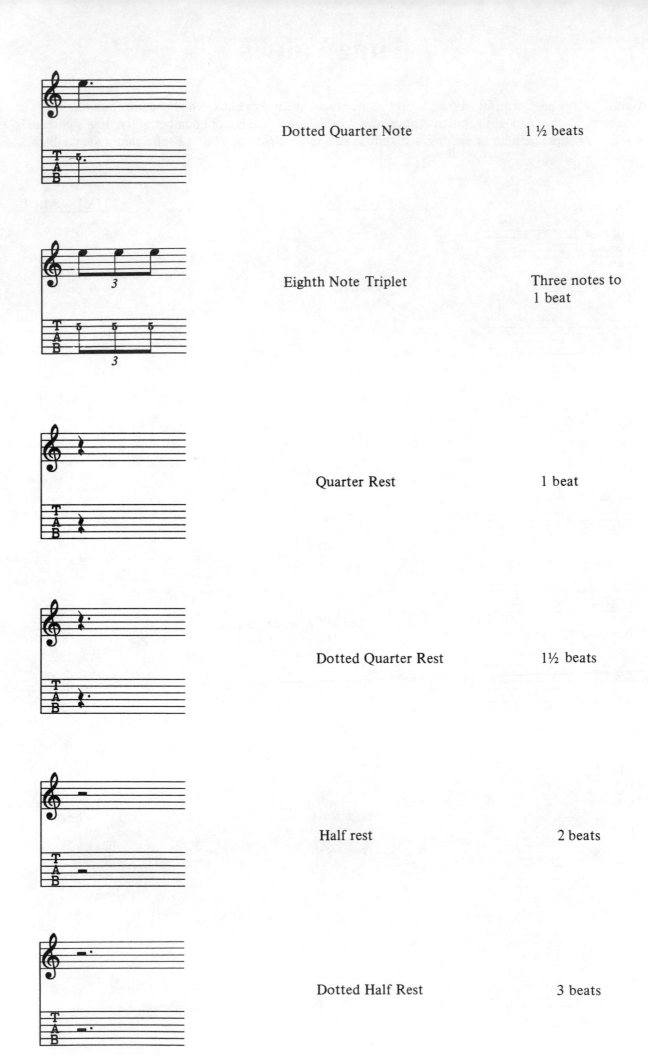

Dotted Quarter Note   1 ½ beats

Eighth Note Triplet   Three notes to 1 beat

Quarter Rest   1 beat

Dotted Quarter Rest   1½ beats

Half rest   2 beats

Dotted Half Rest   3 beats

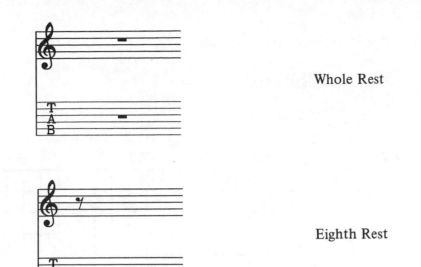

| Whole Rest | 4 beats |
| Eighth Rest | ½ beat |

The Blues Progression

One of the most popular forms of the blues is the 12-bar blues progression. The term *progression* refers to a series of chords. *Twelve-bar* means the progression is 12 measures long. The three chords used in the basic 12-bar progression are the I, IV, and V chords. The I chord (sometimes called the *tonic*) has the same letter name as the key in which you are playing. For example, the I chord in the key of E is E. The IV chord (subdominant) has the letter name which is four steps up the major scale from the I chord. The IV chord in the key of E is A. The V chord (dominant) has the same letter name as the fifth step up the major scale from the I chord. The V chord in the key of E is B. The following chart shows the I, IV, and V chords in the different keys. The more common keys are shown first.

Key

I (Tonic)	IV (Subdominant)	V (Dominant)
E	A	B
A	D	E
D	G	A
G	C	D
C	F	G
F	B♭	C
B♭	E♭	F
E♭	A♭	B♭
A♭	D♭	E♭
D♭	G♭	A♭
B	E	F♯
F♯	B	C♯
G♭	C♭	D♭

The diagrams below show some of the basic chords used to play the blues.

Basic Chords

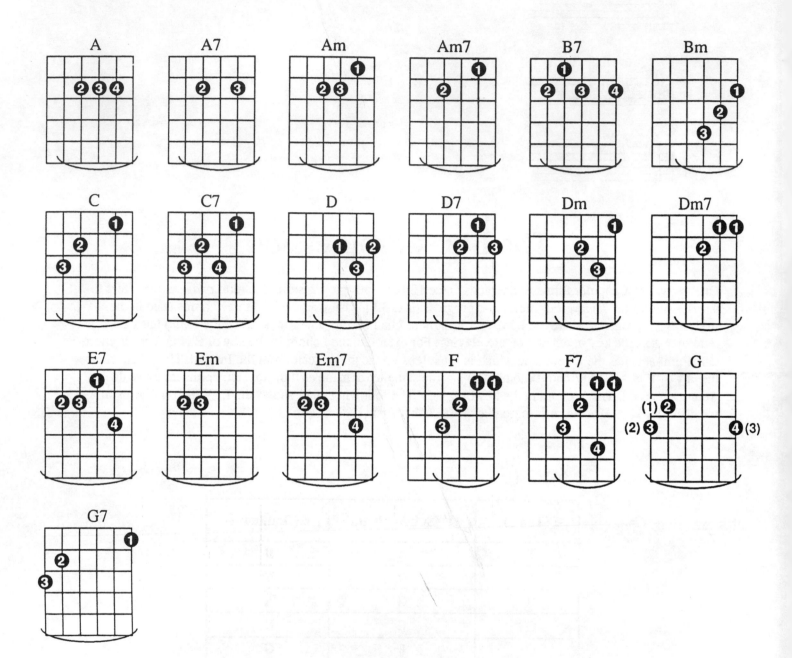

The formula for building the basic 12-bar blues progression is: four measures of the I chord, two measures of the IV chord, two measures of the I chord, one measure of the V chord, one measure of the IV chord, and two measures of the I chord. It's very common to replace the last measure of the I chord with a V chord if the progression is going to be repeated. This last measure is sometimes called the *turnaround*. The advantage of knowing the Roman numeral formula is that, by plugging in the correct I, IV, and V chords, you can play the blues in any key.

The following exercise is the basic 12-bar blues progression. Notice that the number of measures that each chord is played fits the blues formula. The chords in parentheses are the chords which would be used to play the blues in the key of E. Seventh chords (7) are commonly used on every chord in the blues because of their dissonant quality.

Play the following progression strumming down four times in each measure. While it may seem overly simple, strumming down four times in a measure was, and is, a fairly popular technique. Accent beats two and four.

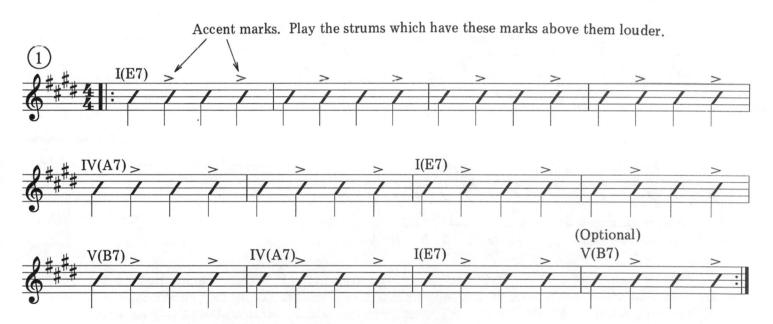

The next progression is a very common variation of the 12-bar blues. The IV chord has been added in the second measure. Remember the V chord in the last measure is optional. This chord can be played if the progression is going to be repeated. If you're not repeating the progression, play the I chord in the last measure. Practice strumming this exercise. In each measure of the progression, play the strum pattern which is written in the first measure. This strum pattern works well when playing songs in 4/4.

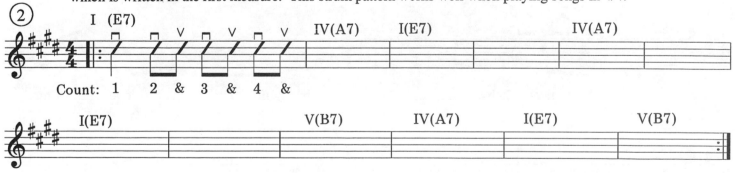

Strum the next progression which is a blues in the key of A. In each measure, use the strum pattern which is written in the first measure. This is another strum pattern which works to accompany songs in 4/4.

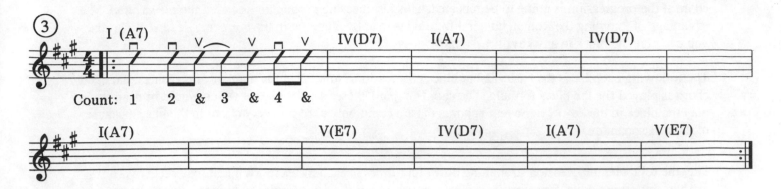

The following *strum patterns* can be used to accompany songs in 4/4. Each pattern takes one measure to complete. Once you decide on which pattern you would like to use for a particular song, play the same pattern in each measure of the song.

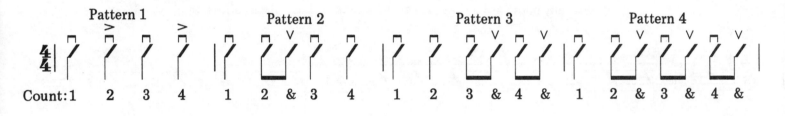

Play the chords to the following song which is a blues in the key of E. In each measure, use the strum pattern which is written above the first measure. You should also practice the song again using some of the other strum patterns for 4/4. The trick is singing the melody which is written while playing the strum pattern. You have to practice the strum pattern enough so that you don't have to think about it while you're singing.

Baby Don't Love Me

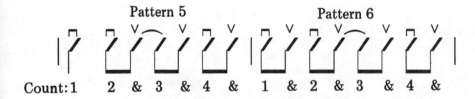

10

but my baby don't love— me.   Feelin' down and lonely.——

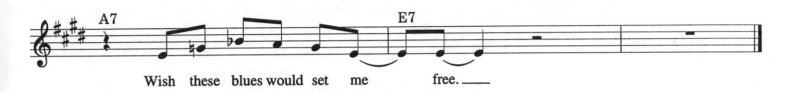

Wish these blues would set me free.——

The next exercise is a blues in 6/8 time. The strum pattern which is written in the first measure is a common strum for 6/8. Use this pattern to play each measure of the progression.

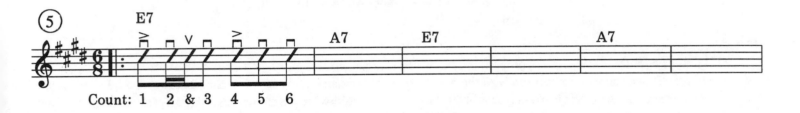

Count: 1   2   &   3   4   5   6

The following exercise is the blues in 12/8 time in the key of E. In each measure, play the strum pattern which is written in the first measure. This is a common strum for 12/8. Notice the accents on beats 1, 4, 7, and 10. Because of the accents, 12/8 should actually feel like four beats in a measure.

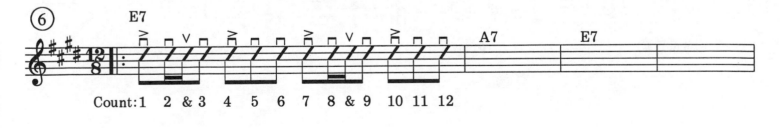

Count:1   2   &   3   4   5   6   7   8   &   9   10   11   12

To play the blues in a minor key, the i and iv chords are minor and the V chord is still a seventh chord. Small Roman numerals indicate minor chords. Practice strumming the following blues in A minor. Use any of the strum patterns for 4/4. Remember to use the same strum pattern in each measure.

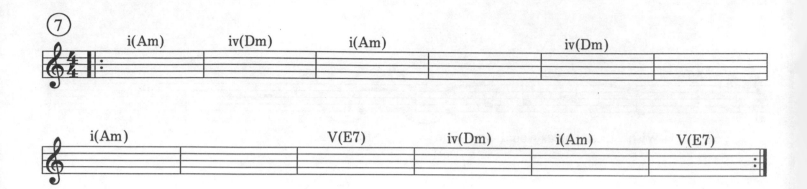

Power Chords

Another popular method of accompanying the blues is to use *power chords* rather than strumming full chords. Power chords are written with the 5 next to the chord name (A5). **Power chords may also be used when the written chord is a seventh (7) chord.** The following diagrams show the A5, D5, and E5 chords. Only two strings are played on each chord. One of the strings played is open. Play the strings quickly so they sound simultaneously. The tablature and notes which are played are written next to each diagram. Hold each chord and play it several times.

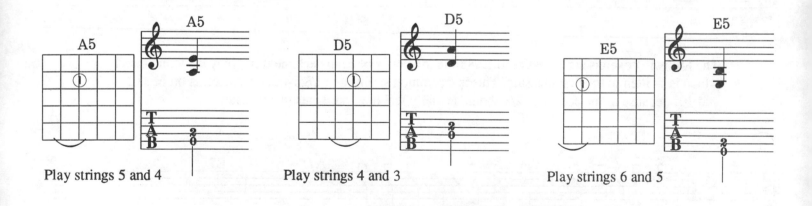

12

A popular way of using power chords for the guitar accompaniment is to play each chord eight times in a measure (two times to each beat). Play the next blues progression which shows how this is done. The eighth note strums are written as two strum bars connected with a beam ( ). This shows that the chord is played two times to each beat (once on the downbeat and once in between the beats). Notice that only downstrokes are used. Be sure to play only two strings on each power chord.

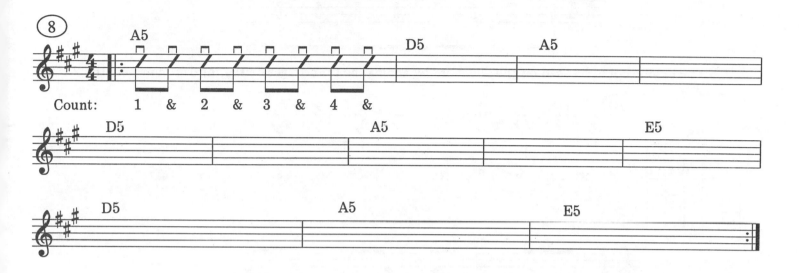

It is very common to play eighth notes (two notes or strums to a beat) to use *shuffle* or *swing* rhythm. This means that, rather than dividing the beat into two equal parts, the beat is divided into a long-short pattern. The eighth notes will sound more like a one-beat triplet with the middle note tied ( ). This gives the music a kind of bouncy feel. **Unless otherwise indicated, all of the solos and accompaniments in this book should be played with this feel.**

Practice exercise number 8 again using swing (or shuffle) rhythm.

A common variation on the power chord involves adding a finger on the third and seventh downstrokes (on the second and fourth beats) of the measure. For example, on the A5 chord, play strings 5 and 4 together four times. Use only downstrokes. On the third stroke, add the left-hand third finger where the "X" is drawn on the diagram below. On the fourth stroke, lift the third finger. Do this twice in each measure.

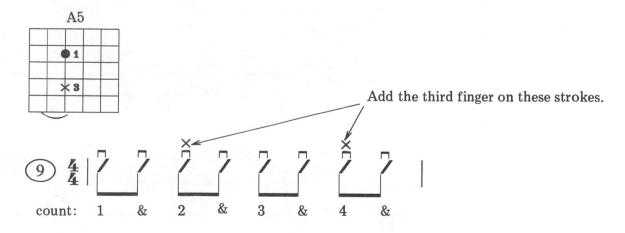

Add the third finger on these strokes.

The following shows the notation and tablature for this technique.

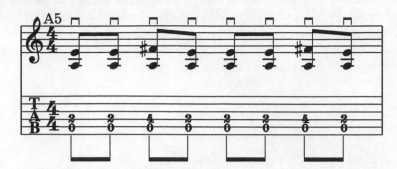

This technique could be used on the D5 chord by adding the third finger on the third string where the "X" is drawn.

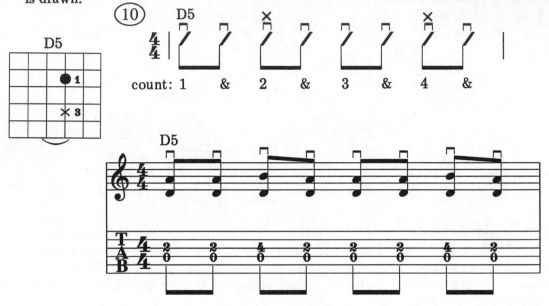

For the E5, add the third finger in the fourth fret on the fifth string.

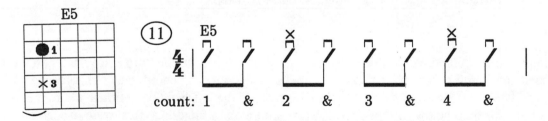

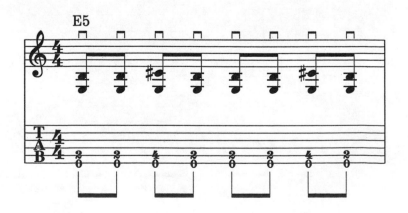

The next exercise uses this variation on the power chords.

In the next song, the guitar accompaniment uses the variation on the power chords. The melody is written on the top staff and the guitar part is written below. Remember, power chords can be used if the written chord is a seventh (7) chord.

Good Mornin' Blues

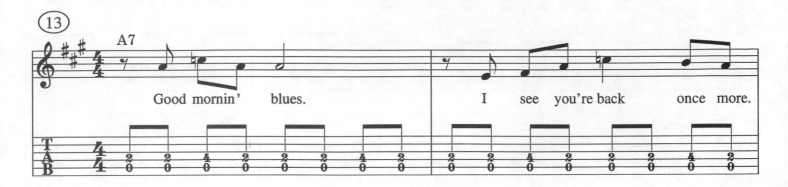

Good mornin' blues.   I see you're back   once more.

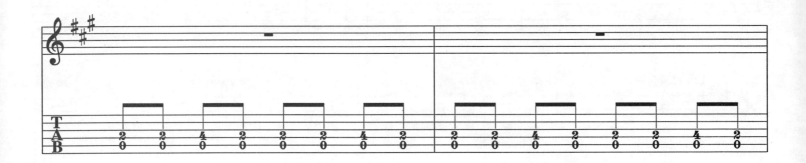

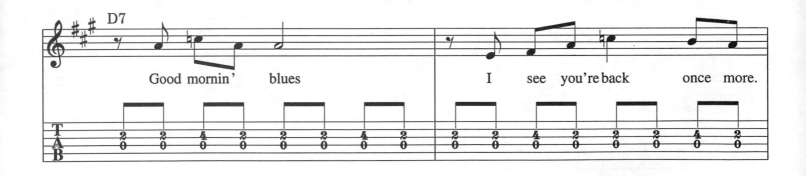

Good mornin' blues   I see you're back   once more.

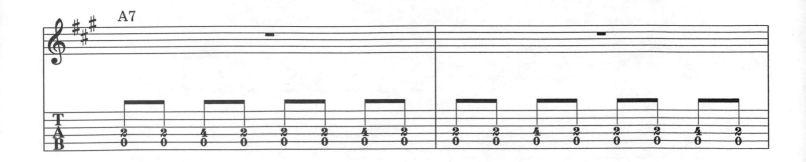

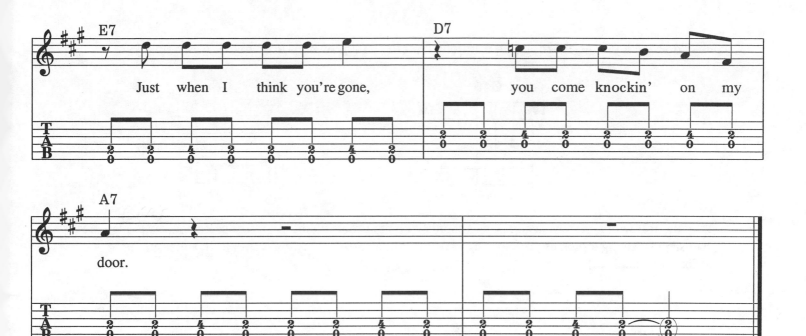

Movable Power Chords

Power chords (two-string chords) can also be played without using open strings. The following diagram shows a power chord which can be played anywhere on the guitar neck. The note with the "R" pointing to it is the "root." The letter name of this note will be the letter name of the power chord. When playing this chord, play only the strings which have fingers on them.

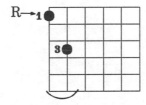

The following chart shows the names of the notes (roots) on the sixth string and the fret numbers in which they are played.

0	1	3	5	7	8	10	12	Fret
E	F	G	A	B	C	D	E	Root name

Power chords may be played on any step of the scale. For example, B5 would have the root in the 7th fret.

B5

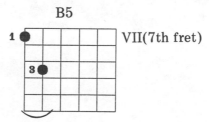

VII(7th fret)

17

To sharp a power chord, move it up one fret; to flat a power chord, move it down one fret.

Play the following exercise using power chords with their roots on the sixth string. Remember to play only two strings. Using a pick or your thumb, play only downstrokes. Play eight strokes in a measure (two strokes to each beat).

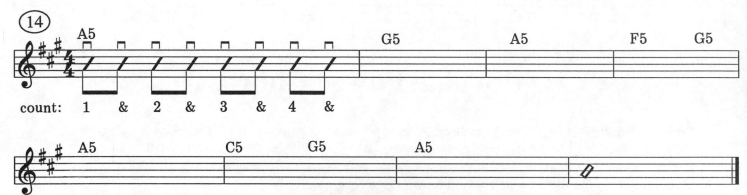

A power chord may also have its root on the fifth string. The following diagram shows the fingering for this type of power chord.

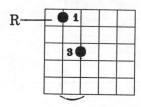

The following chart shows the fret numbers for the root names on the fifth string.

0	2	3	5	7	8	10	12	Fret number
A	B	C	D	E	F	G	A	Root name

Drawn below are two examples of power chords with their roots on the fifth string.

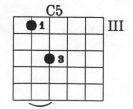

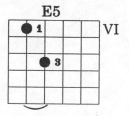

As with the other power chords, sharp the chord by moving the pattern up one fret, and flat the chord by moving it down one fret.
Practice the following progressions using power chords with roots on the fifth string.

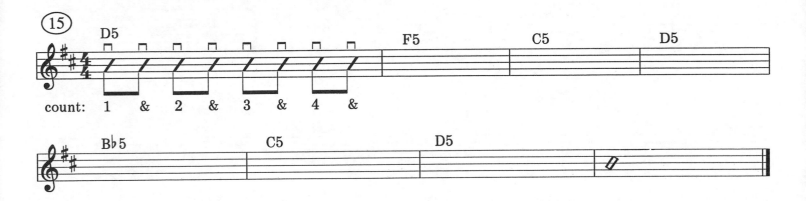

Play the following blues progression which uses power chords with their roots on the sixth and fifth strings. By combining the two different groups of power chords, the different chords can be played close to each other. To help you know which power chord to use, those with the "R6" have their roots on the sixth string, and those with their roots on the fifth string are indicated with "R5." Play eight downstrokes in a measure.

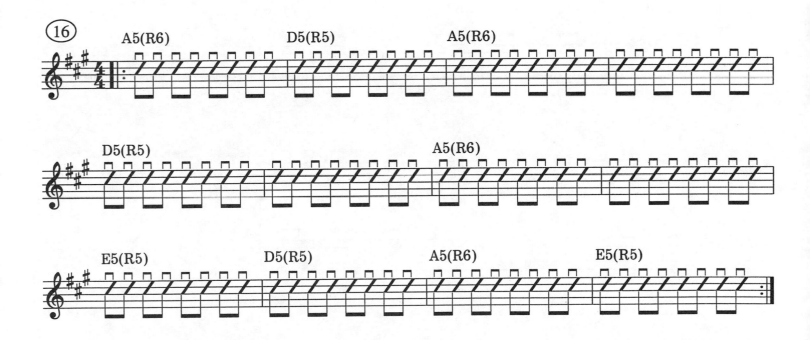

"Movable power chords" can be modified by adding a finger. The following blues progression is in the key of A and shows how this would be done. The fourth finger is added on beats two and four. Remember, these power chords can be used for the accompaniment when the written chord is a major or a 7th chord.

Barre Chords

When a chord has a finger which lies (bars) across all of the strings, it is called a "barre chord." By using the following charts, you will be able to figure out dozens of chords. The numbers at the beginning of each category indicate in which fret to place the "bar finger" (the finger which lies across the strings). The letters under the numbers show which letter name the chord will have when the bar finger is in that fret.

The first category of barre chords has the root (note which names the chord) on the sixth string. The chart above the diagrams shows the names and fret numbers for those notes (roots). The patterns show how to finger the various types of chords (i.e., major, 7th, etc.). To flat a barre chord, move the entire pattern down one fret. To sharp a barre chord, move the pattern up one fret. Because the B♭ root is in the sixth fret, the B♭7 chord would be played with the bar finger in the sixth fret and by holding the fingering for a 7th chord.

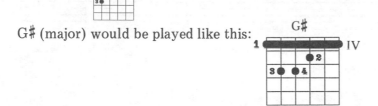

G♯ (major) would be played like this:

Major chords are those which have only a letter name written such as: G, C, D, and A. Major chords may also be sharped or flatted.

The chord patterns which are drawn are chords that are commonly used in playing the blues.

First Category

1	3	5	7	8	10	12	Fret
F	G	A	B	C	D	E	Root (chord letter name)

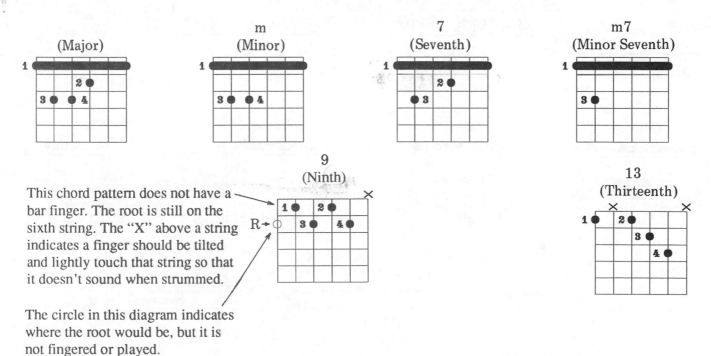

This chord pattern does not have a bar finger. The root is still on the sixth string. The "X" above a string indicates a finger should be tilted and lightly touch that string so that it doesn't sound when strummed.

The circle in this diagram indicates where the root would be, but it is not fingered or played.

Practice the following exercise using barre chords from the first category. Play each chord as a barre chord. Use the strum pattern which is written in the first measure to play each measure of the exercise.

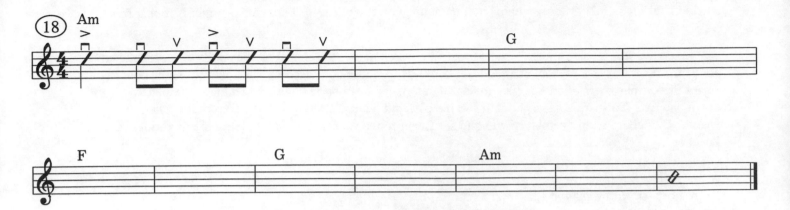

Second Category

By knowing two groups of barre chords, chord changes may be kept closer together and more convenient. The second category of barre chords has the root on the fifth string. In the chart above the diagrams, the numbers show in which fret to place the bar finger. The letters tell what the name of the chord will be when the bar finger is placed in that fret. The diagrams show fingerings for the various types of chords. Because the root D would be in the fifth fret, the D7 chord would be played like this:

Because the root is on the fifth string, the second category of barre chords will generally sound best if only five strings are strummed.

2	3	5	7	8	10	12	Fret
B	C	D	E	F	G	A	Root (chord letter name)

The "X" above the string in these diagrams means that string is not played.

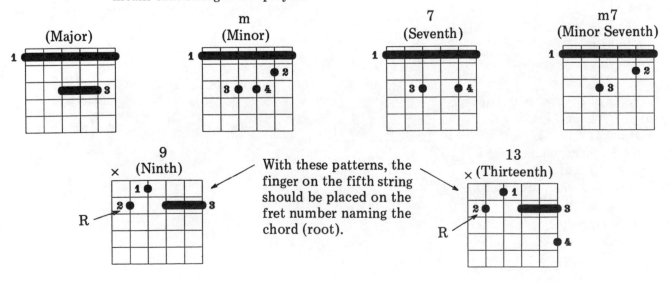

With these patterns, the finger on the fifth string should be placed on the fret number naming the chord (root).

Practice the following progression using barre chords from the second category. Use the strum pattern which is written in the first measure throughout the exercise. Play each chord as a barre chord.

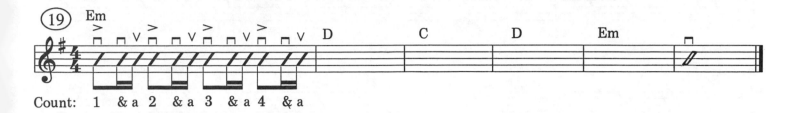

Count: 1 & a 2 & a 3 & a 4 & a

When playing the following blues progression, play each chord as a barre chord. You should combine both categories of barre chords. First, strum down four times in each measure. You could then use the strum patterns which are presented earlier in this book.

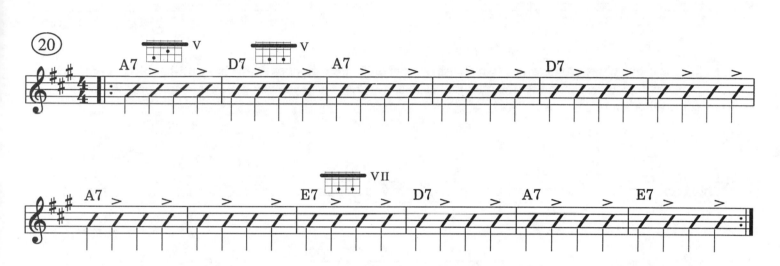

The following pattern for a seventh chord can also move up and down the neck. Like the second category of barre chords, it has its root on the fifth string. The "X" above the sixth string means that string is not played, and the "X" above the first string indicates to tilt the first finger of the left hand and bump the first string, making it dead. The first string is not heard when the chord is strummed.

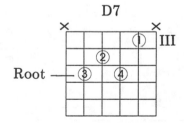

Play the following blues progression which uses this new seventh chord pattern and barre chords.

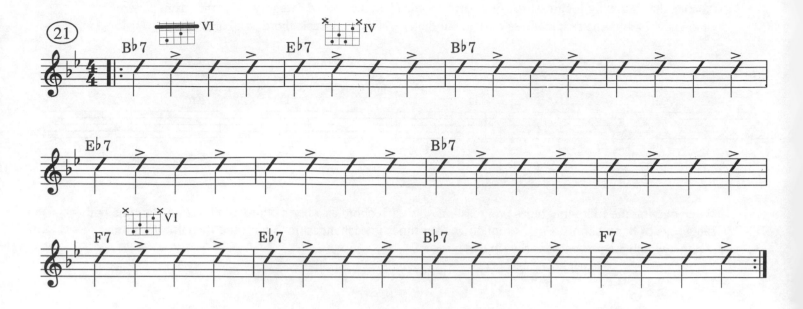

The next two blues progressions (which use barre chords) are variations on the basic 12-bar blues. First, play the exercises strumming down four times in a measure. Then, you could play the same progressions using other strum patterns for 4/4.

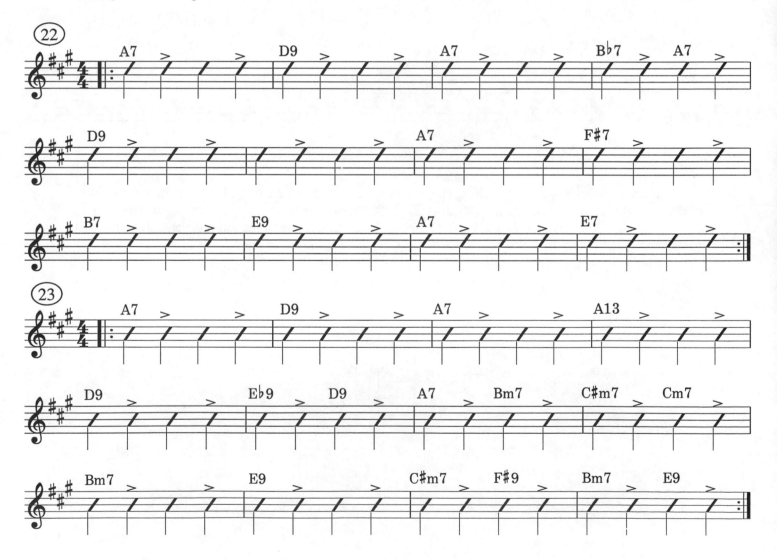

Strum the chords to the following blues song using barre chords and the new seventh chord pattern. This song is in 12/8 time. Use the strum pattern which is written above the first measure for each measure of the song. Be sure to play the accents. Practice changing the chords smoothly.

Be Your Puppet

The Tie

A loop which connects two of the *same* notes is called a *tie*. When a tie is written, pick the first note and let it ring through the time value of the second note. **Do not play the second note.**

Play the following solo which has some ties.

26

Hammer-On

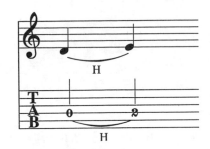

A very effective tool in playing blues guitar is the *hammer-on*. A hammer-on is written as two different notes connected with a loop and an "H" is written by the loop. The second note will be higher than the first. To play a hammer-on, pick the first note and, without picking the string again, push a finger hard on the second (higher) note. The second note should sound clear without picking the string again. The time value of the two notes should be the same as if both notes were picked.

Practice the following solo which contains *hammer-ons*.

Pull-Off

Another effective tool used in blues guitar is the *pull-off*. A pull-off is written as two different notes connected with a loop and a "P" is written near the loop. To play a pull-off, pick the first (higher) note and without picking the string again, pull the left-hand finger off of the string on an angle so the left-hand finger actually picks the string and the second note is sounded. Do not pick the second note. If both notes are fingered (the second note is not an open string), make sure that both fingers are down before you pull the finger off of the first note.

Play the next solo which contains pull-offs.

28

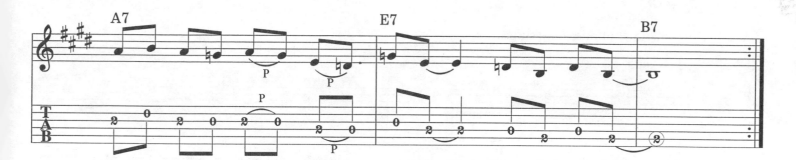

The Slide

A slide is indicated with a slanted line written before a note and an "sl." is written by the line. If the line slants up to the note, slide from two frets below to the written note. The slide should be done quickly. Be sure to keep the left-hand finger pushing on the string while you slide.

If the line slants down to the note, slide from two frets above to the written note.

If two notes are connected with a slanted line, pick the first note and then without picking the string again, slide the same finger on the string to the second note.

29

The next solo contains some slides.

The Bend

A bend is written with a curved arrow next to the note. To play a bend, first pick the string and then bend it upward. Depending on the gauge string you are using, you may have to push with more than one finger to do the bend. If "1/2" is written by the curved arrow, bend the note so it sounds 1/2 step (one fret) higher than the written note. If "full" is written, bend the note so it sounds one whole step (two frets) higher than the written note.

Play the next solo which contains some bends.

31

Vibrato

One of the most commonly used effects in blues soloing is the use of *vibrato*. Vibrato can be done in several ways. A subtle vibrato can be played by rotating on the tip of the left-hand finger from side to side (left to right). This is a smooth-sounding vibrato. There should be no pressure on the back of the neck with the left-hand thumb. The shaking motion should come from the left elbow. Imagine the very tip of the left-hand finger being glued to the string, and then move the hand from left to right, pivoting on the tip of the finger. Practice playing a few notes with this vibrato.

A more dramatic type of vibrato is commonly used in playing the blues. This type of vibrato is done by bending the string back and forth quickly with the left-hand finger. The left hand should touch the neck at the base of the first finger and pivot back and forth. The string is bent by turning the wrist and forearm rather than pulling with the finger. This type of vibrato is *sometimes* indicated with a wavy line written above the note ( ). Even if it's not indicated, this type of vibrato may be used on long and repeated notes.

Play the next solo using the more dramatic (or stronger) vibrato where indicated and on the long and repeated notes.

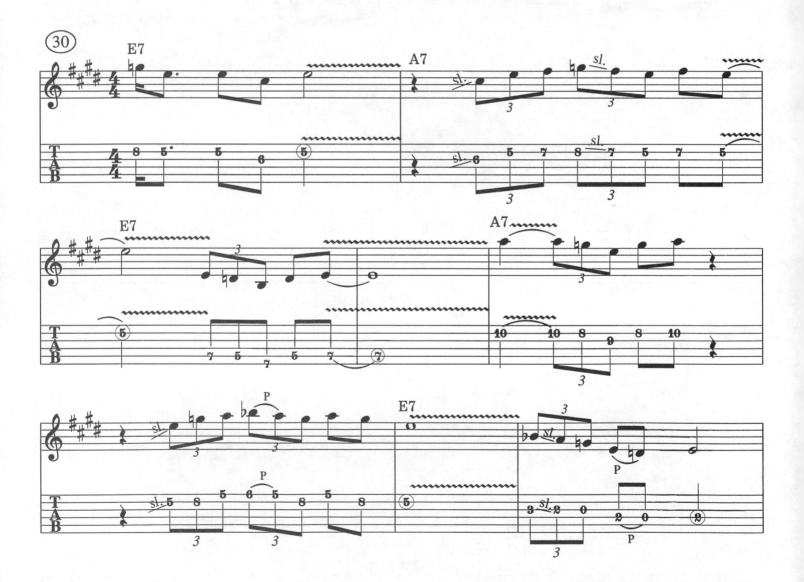

Turnarounds

A turnaround is a group of notes or chords which are played in the last one or two measures of the blues progression. They signal that the progression is going to be repeated, or in other words it will "turn around." A turnaround introduces the first measure. Some turnarounds are very popular and are borrowed by many blues players. They are a very important part of the blues. Many of the turnarounds used by the early blues guitarists are still popular and used today.

Written below are some of the more popular turnarounds used in the keys of E and A. Written in parentheses, above each turnaround, is the key for which that turnaround will work. Turnarounds also make great introductions for the blues progression. You will see them used on many of the solos and songs from here on in this book.

If two notes are played together which are not on adjacent strings, the pick can be used to play the bottom note and the right-hand second finger could be used to play the top note. Or, the right-hand thumb and first or second finger could be used to play the entire turnaround.

Notice the use of strum bar with the notes and tablature. Strum the chord which is written above the measure.

34

The next two songs contain turnarounds. So they can be easily seen, the turnarounds have squares around them.

In the song "Stay Away From Mine," use the strum pattern which is written above the first measure for each measure of the song.

Stay Away From Mine

In "Worn Out Shoes," the vocal melody is written in standard notation and the guitar accompaniment is written in the tablature. The turnarounds have been written in both the standard notation and the tablature. Notice a turnaround has been used for the introduction. Power chords have been used for the accompaniment. Be sure to use *swing (shuffle)* rhythm.

Worn Out Shoes

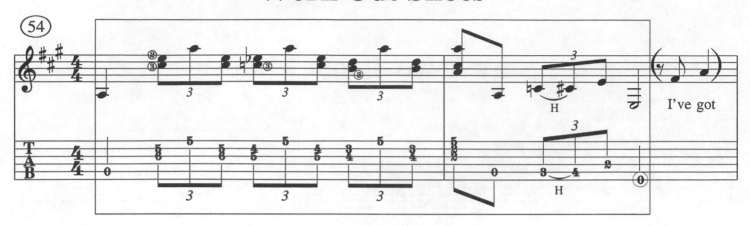

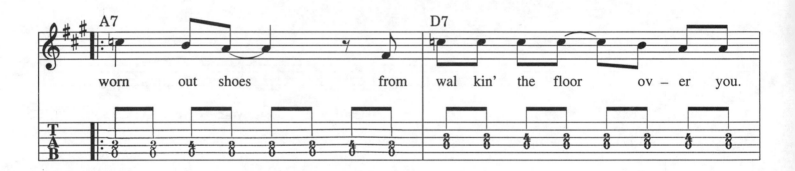

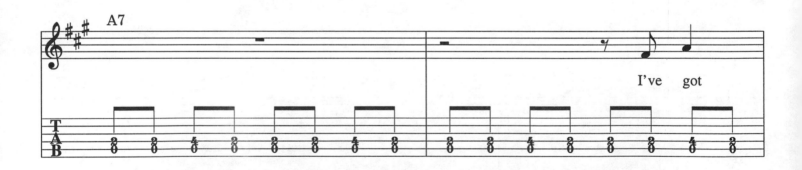

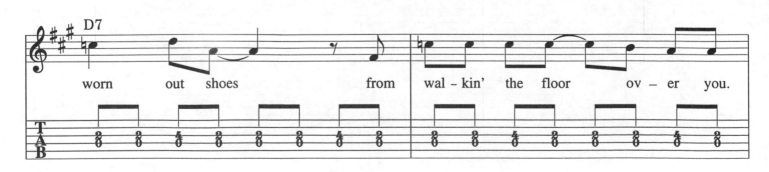

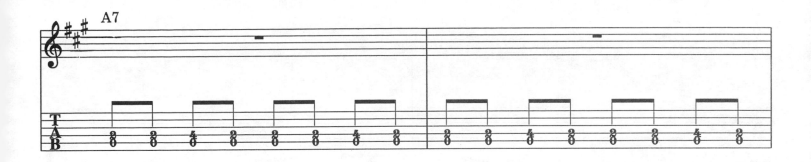

The next two solos also contain turnarounds.

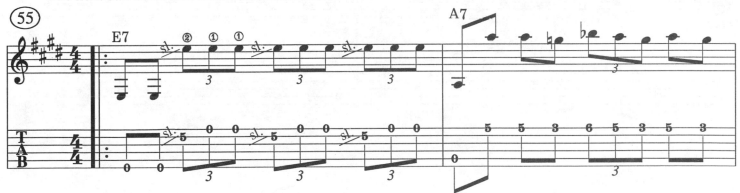

Fill-Ins

A fill-in is a group of notes (or chords) which are played when there is a pause in the vocal part. It's very common for this to happen on the **third and fourth measures,** and also **on the seventh and eighth measures** of the 12-bar blues progression. A fill-in can also be played in the last two measures of the progression in place of a turnaround. The notes used for fill-ins come from the blues scale.

The next song contains some fill-ins. The guitar accompaniment is written in the tablature and the vocal part in standard notation. The fill-ins are written in the tablature. So they can be easily seen, the fill-ins have squares around them.

Beg, Steal Or Borrow

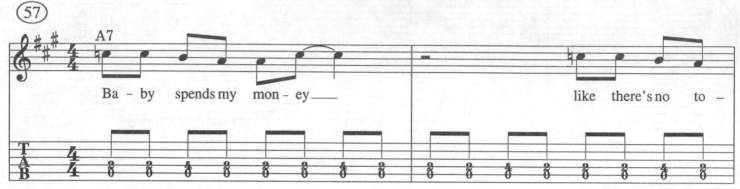

44

mor - row.

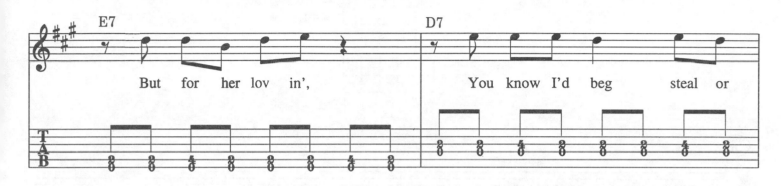

But for her lov in', You know I'd beg steal or

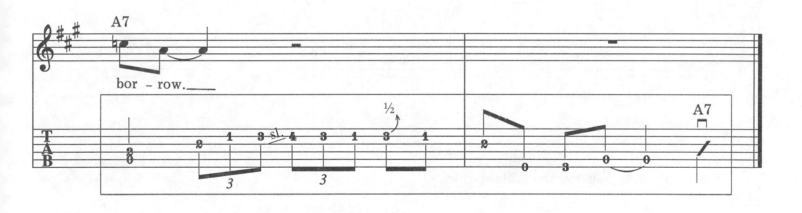

bor - row.____

The Blues Scale

The diagram below shows the blues scale for the key of E. A blues scale contains a root (note which names the scale), ♭3, 4, ♭5, ♮5, and ♭7 steps of a major scale. The empty circles on the diagram indicate to play open strings. When the scale pattern is moved up the neck, these notes are played with the left-hand first finger. Below the diagram are the notes in standard notation and the tablature for the E blues scale. Practice playing up and down the scale. When soloing, the fingerings for the scale may change depending upon the order of the notes in the solo.

The E Blues Scale

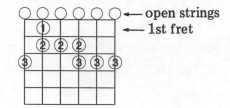

The following solo uses the E blues scale.

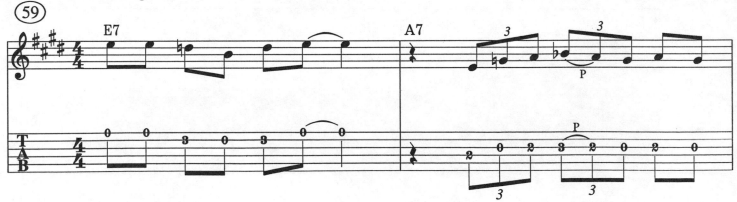

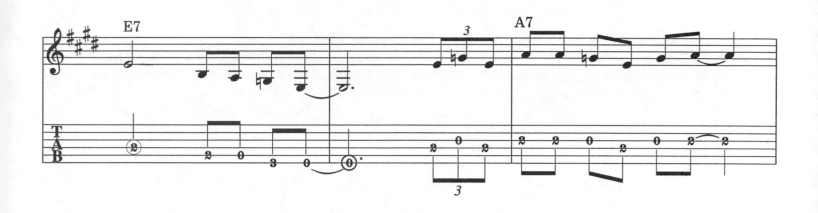

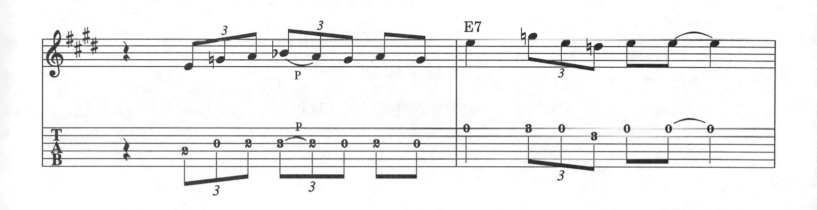

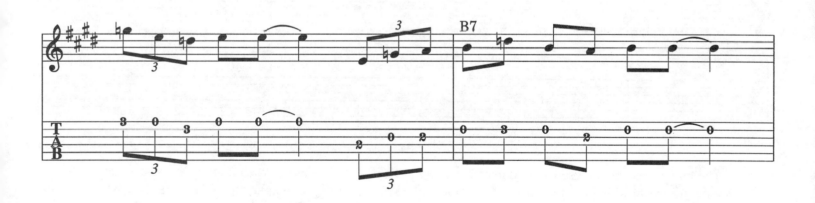

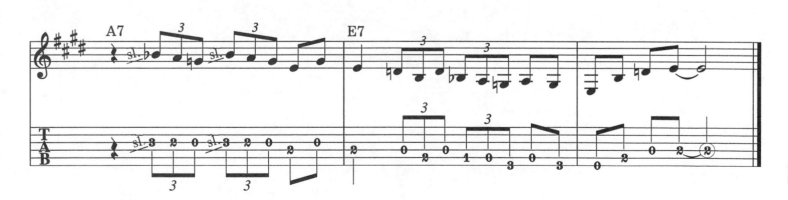

47

Like barre chords, this scale can be moved anywhere on the neck and begin in any fret. The note with the "R" pointing to it is the *root*. The letter name of this note is the letter name of the scale. By placing the root on different notes, you can play the blues scale in any key. The following chart shows the fret numbers for the roots on the sixth string.

Fret	0	1	2	3	4	5	6	7	8	9	10	11	12
Root Name	E	F	F# Gb	G	G# Ab	A	A# Bb	B	C	C# Db	D	D# Eb	E

The next diagram shows the G blues scale. It would be a G blues scale because the root is on the sixth string, third fret (G).

The G Blues Scale

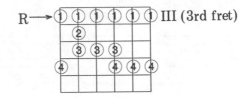

The blues scale can be used to solo over 7th, minor, m7, 9, and 13 chords. When improvising a solo, use the blues scale which has the same letter name as the key in which you are playing. **When the chords change in the progression, it is not necessary to change the scale. The** *key scale* **(the scale with the same letter name as the first chord in the progression) can be used to improvise through the entire progression.** After playing the written solos in this book, try creating your own improvised solos to blues progressions.

The next solo is a blues in the key of G. The blues scale used for the solo has the root on the sixth string, third fret.

The next diagram shows an upper extension of the E blues scale. The standard notation and tablature for this scale are below the diagram. Like the other blues scale you've learned, this pattern can be moved up the neck and used for other keys.

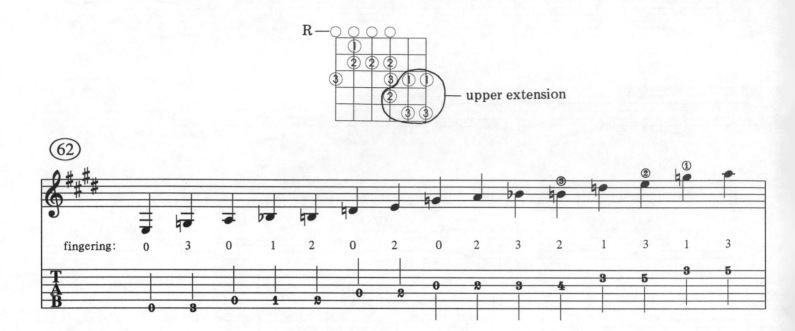

upper extension

The following solo uses the upper extension of the E blues scale.

"Swamp Blues" is a solo which uses combinations of the basic E blues scale and the upper extension.

Swamp Blues

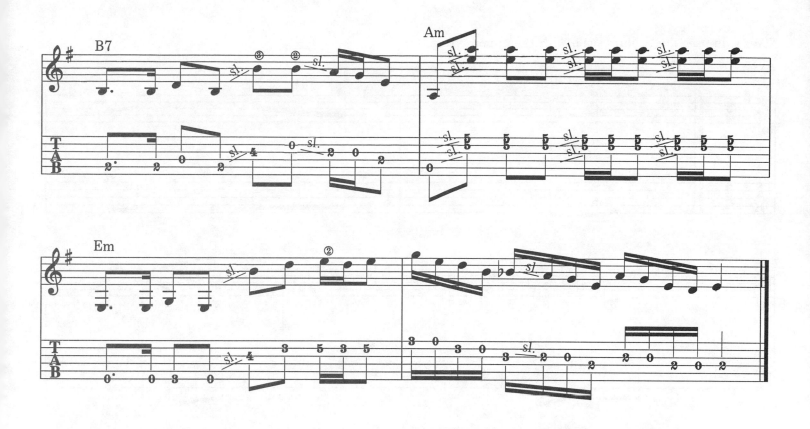

The next diagram shows the G blues scale with the upper extension. The root is in the sixth string, third fret (G).

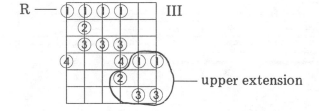

This solo uses the G blues scale with the upper extension.

The blues scale can also be played with the **root on the fifth string.** The diagram below shows the blues scale with the root on the fifth string, open. This would be the A blues scale because the fifth string open is named A. The notes and tablature for the A blues scale are written below the diagram. The empty circles indicate open strings.

The A Blues Scale

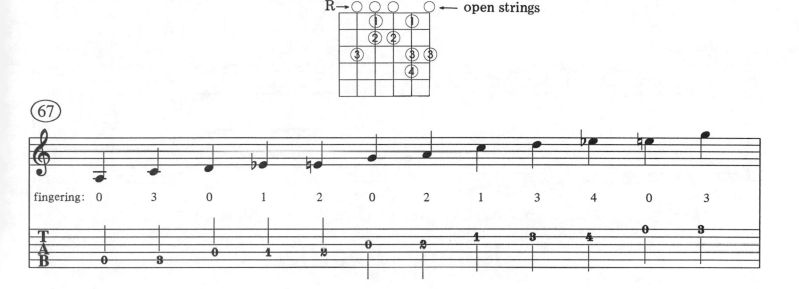

The next solo uses the A blues scale with the root on the fifth string, open. This solo uses even eighth notes rather than the shuffle rhythm.

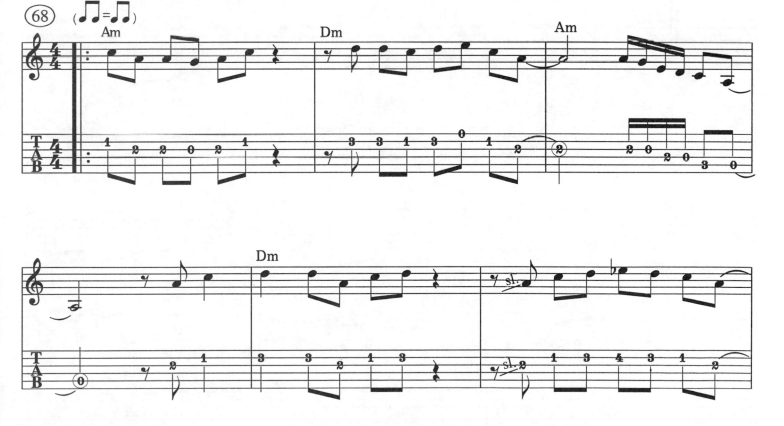

55

"Jimmy's Shuffle" also uses the A blues scale. *Swing (shuffle)* rhythm is used in this solo.

Jimmy's Shuffle

56

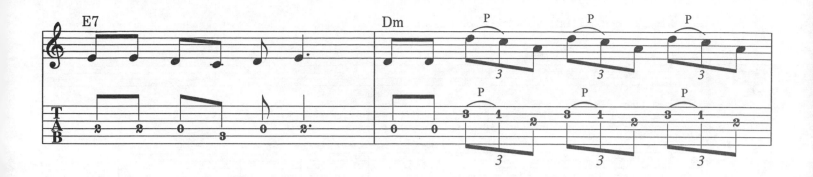

Like the blues scale with the root on the sixth string, the blues scale with the root on the fifth string can be positioned anywhere on the neck. The following chart shows the locations of the root names on the fifth string.

Fret	0	1	2	3	4	5	6	7	8	9	10	11	12
Root Name	A	A♯ B♭	B	C	C♯ D♭	D	D♯ E♭	E	F	F♯ G♭	G	G♯ A♭	A

The diagram below is the C blues scale because the pattern is positioned so the root is on the fifth string, third fret which is C. The notes and tablature for the C blues scale are written below the diagram.

The C Blues Scale

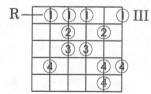

57

The next solo in 12/8 time uses the C blues scale.

The blues scale with the root on the fifth string also has an upper extension. The next diagram shows the A blues scale with the upper extension. It is the A blues scale because the root is on the fifth string, open (A). The notes and tablature for the A blues scale with the upper extension are written below the diagram.

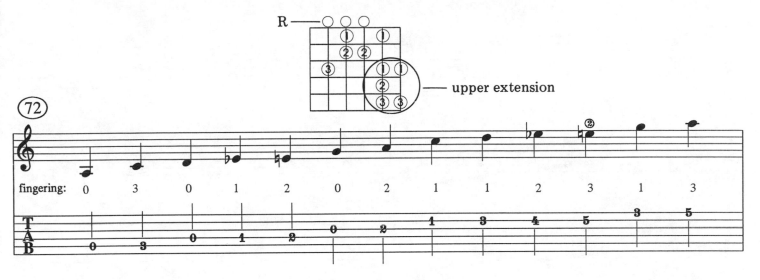

The next solo uses the A blues scale with the upper extension.

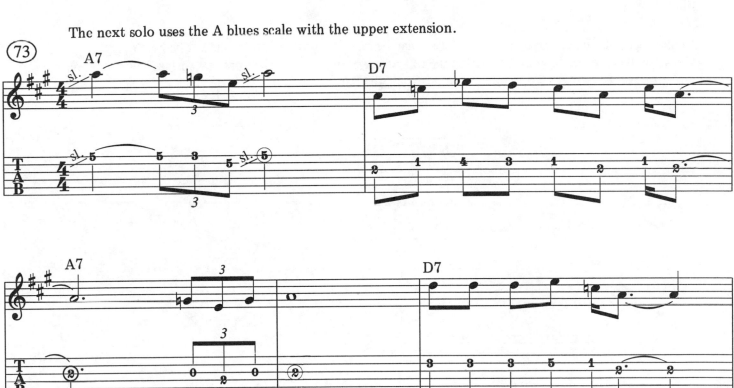

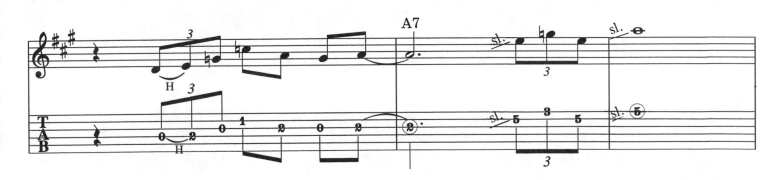

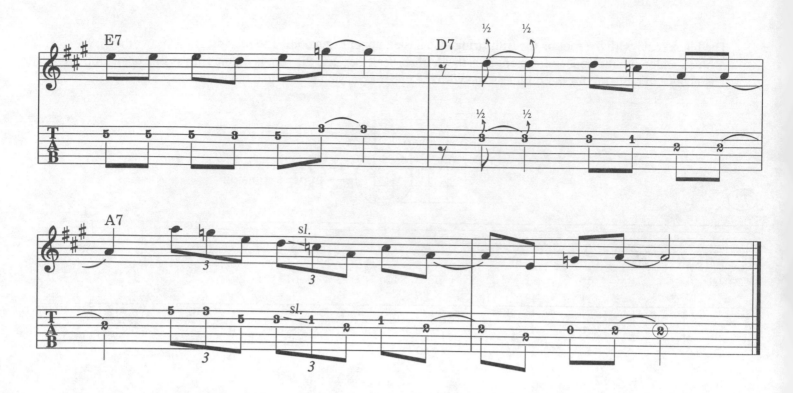

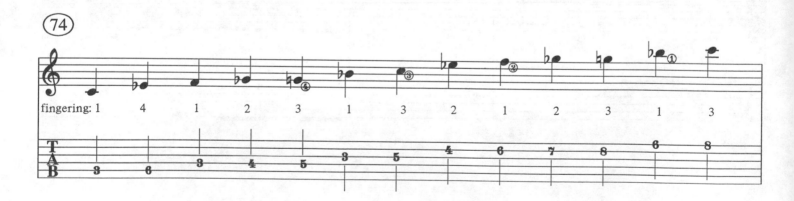

Remember, this scale with its upper extension can be moved anywhere on the neck. The next diagram shows the C blues scale with the root on the fifth string, third fret, and the upper extension. The notes and tablature for the C blues scale are written below the diagram.

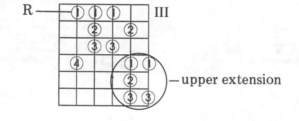

— upper extension

The following solo uses the C blues scale with the upper extension.

Using The Capo

A capo is a clamp which attaches to the guitar neck and raises the pitch of the notes and chords. By using the capo, all of the solos and/or accompaniments in this book can be played in any key. For every fret the capo is moved up the neck, the pitch of the chords and/or notes is raised 1/2 step. For example, with the capo in the second fret, a song or solo which is written in the key of A would sound like you're playing it in the key of B. The notes and chords are fingered as though the first fret up from the capo is the first fret on the guitar. Make sure the capo is placed next to the fret wire but not on top of it. This will prevent the strings from buzzing when they are played open. Try playing some of the songs and solos from the book and experiment with placing the capo in different frets to change the key. Play the songs and the solos the same as you did without the capo only imagine the first fret up from the capo is the first fret on the guitar.

Double Stops

A *double stop* occurs when two strings are played at one time. When using the pick, be sure to play the two strings quickly so they sound at the same time. The following diagram shows some common double stops for the key of E. The lines connecting the circles show which notes can be played together. Below the diagram, the double stops for the key of E are written in standard notation and tablature. Like barre chords and the blues scales, the double stop patterns can be moved around the guitar neck so they will work for any key. This is done by placing the root (the note with the "R" pointing to it) on the desired key.

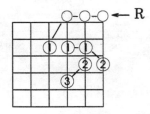

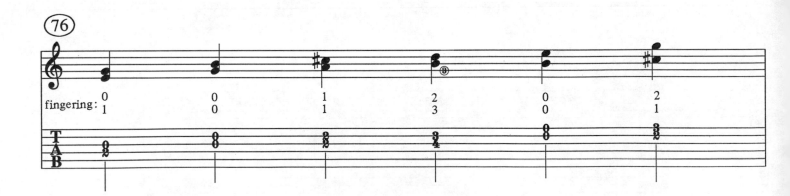

The following solos contain double stops for the key of E.

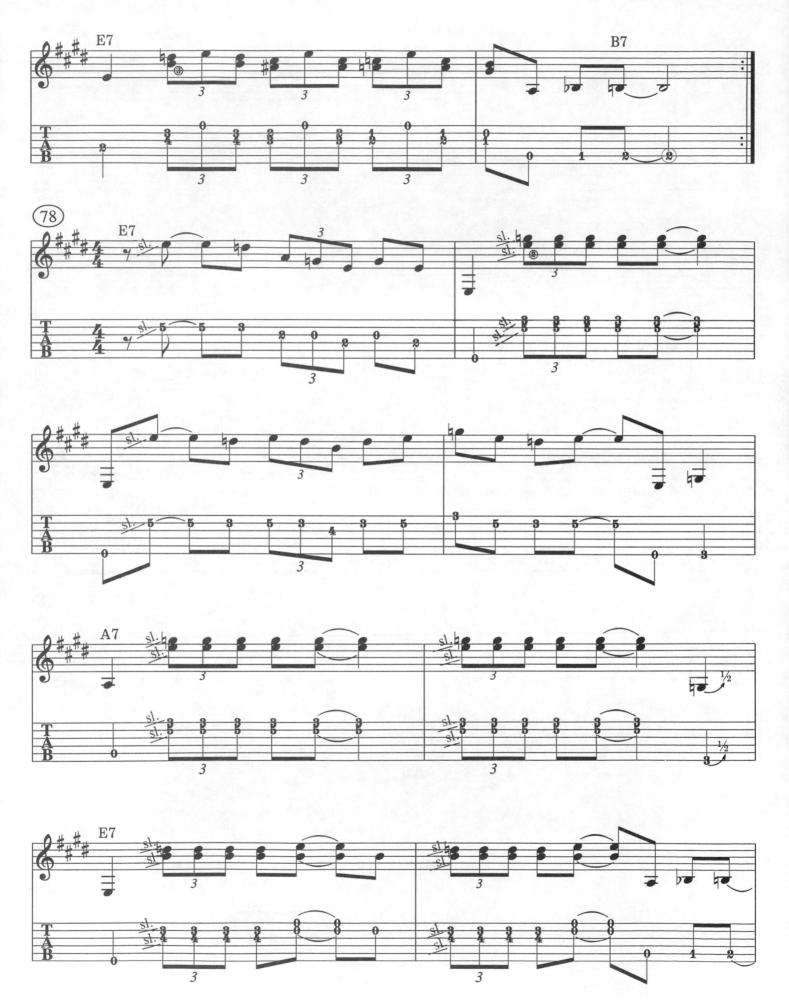

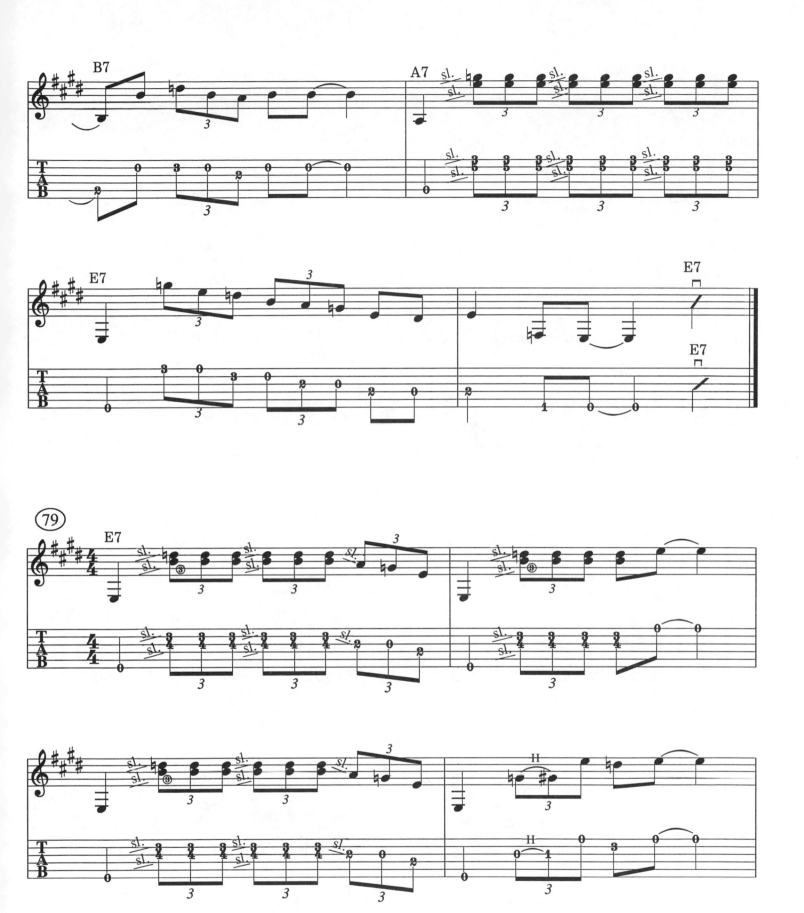

Common Blues Licks

Licks are groups of notes which have a "catchy" sound and are often repeated over and over in a solo. You'll probably recognize the sound of these licks because they were (and are) used by many popular artists. When the licks are combined with the blues scale, the solo will take on a professional, "classy" sound. The following licks work against the E7 or A7 chords. The chord for which the licks will work is written above the lick in parentheses. Practice playing each lick several times.

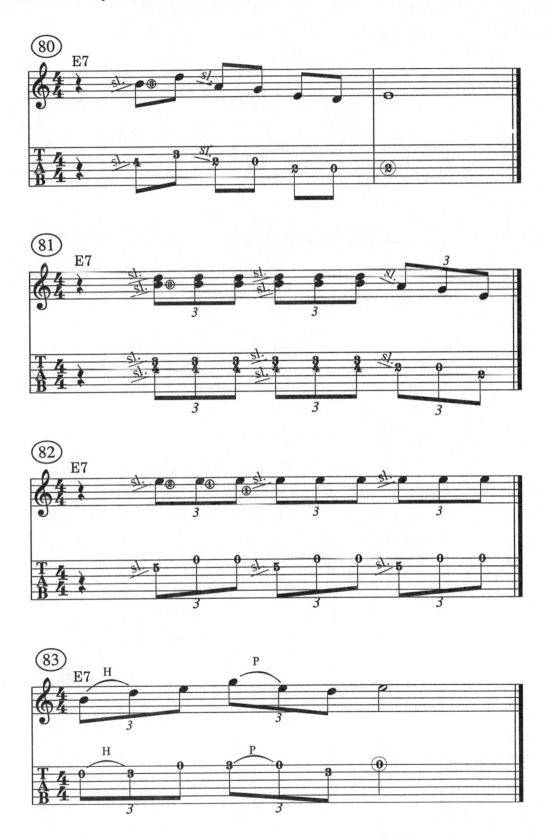

67

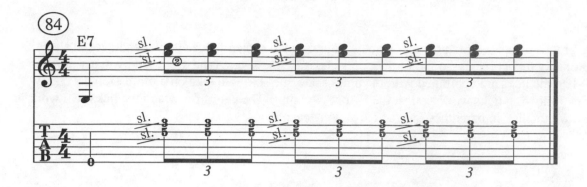

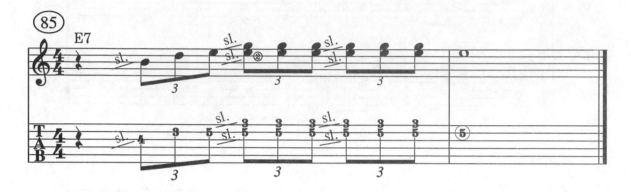

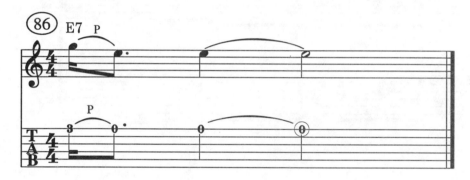

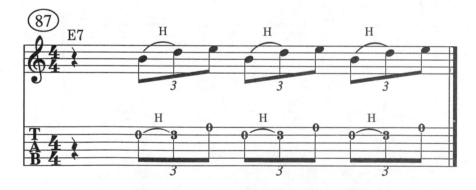

Trill: With a series of hammer-ons and pull-offs, play from the first note to the note in parentheses. The trill should last for the time value of the first note.

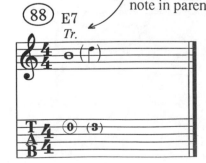

68

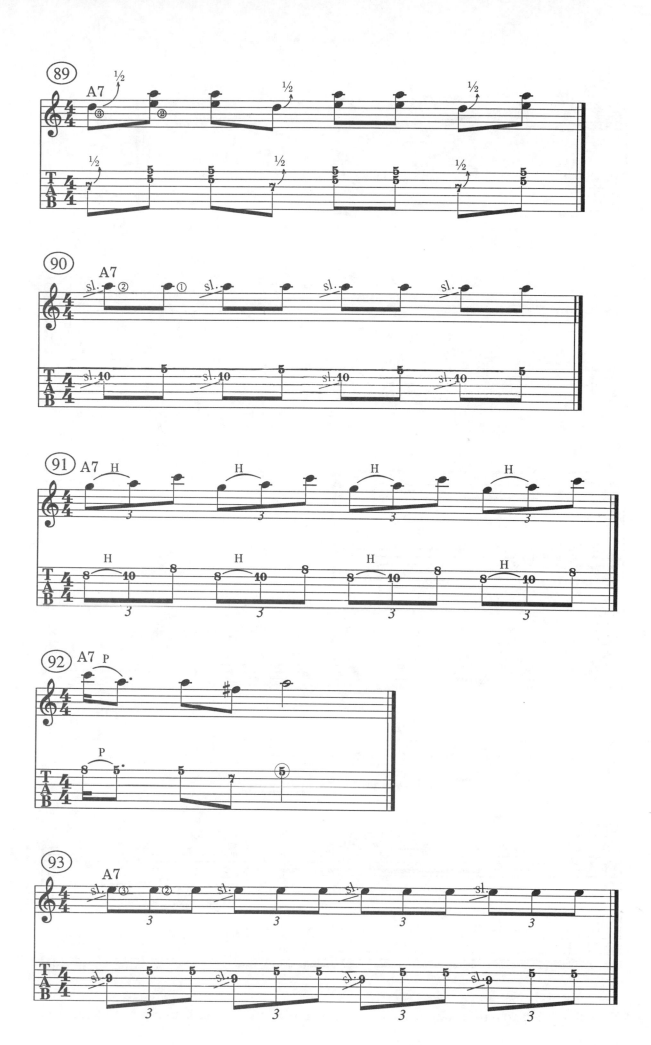

Try improvising your own solos in the keys of E and A and using these licks as a part of your solo.

Bass Line Accompaniments

Another device used to accompany the blues is the use of a repeated bass line. Rather than strumming chords, the guitarist plays bass notes for the accompaniment. The notes which are used for the bass line are taken from the blues scale. Notice that the bass line accompaniment begins each measure with the note which has the letter name of the chord for that measure. Also, notice that the order in which the notes are played is the same in each measure. This creates an accompaniment *pattern*.

The next exercise shows a bass line which could be used for an accompaniment in the key of A minor. In this exercise, play the eighth notes evenly rather than with a shuffle rhythm.

You're The Cure

The following blues song has the vocal melody on the top and the guitar bass line accompaniment written in the tablature. Use even eighth notes for the accompaniment.

Building A Blues Solo

After you have learned the blues scales, try creating your own improvised solos. This may seem difficult at first because, although you know the notes in the scale which you can use, you may not be sure of how to mix them up. Here are a few guidelines that will help you in building your own solos:

1. **Work with only a few notes of the scale.** Don't try to use every note in the scale in your solo.
2. **Avoid a series of large skips.** Although some skips sound good, try to play a lot of the solo using the notes in *scale order* (playing each note of the scale without skipping).
3. **Build your solo on one or two ideas.** Your idea can be a *melody* or a *rhythm*. Use the same melody or rhythm repeatedly in the solo. Try to keep your ideas short and simple.

In the next solo, the first two measures contain a melody *idea* (referred to in the solo as the *melodic idea*) which is used again in the solo. So that it can be easily seen, the melodic idea has a square around it. Notice the idea from measures one and two is repeated again in measures five and six. This would be a common place to repeat the idea. Also notice that only a small portion of the E blues scale has been used for the solo and, although there are some skips, much of the solo uses the notes in scale order moving back and forth through the scale.

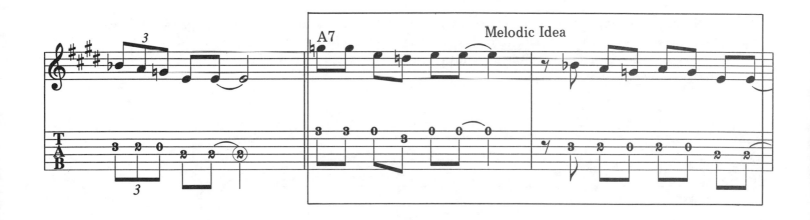

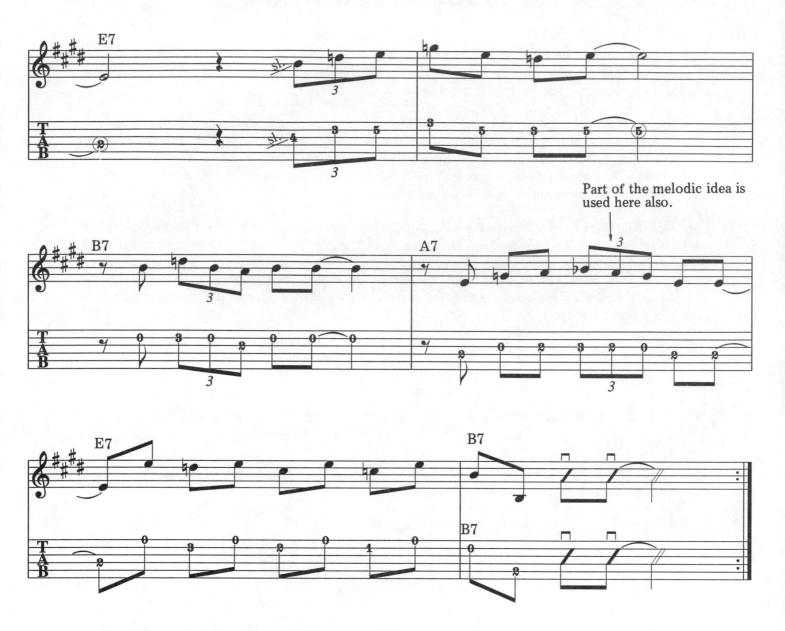

Part of the melodic idea is
used here also.

In the next solo, a rhythmic idea (a certain rhythm) is repeated in the solo. Though the notes are different, the same rhythm is repeated in the solo. So you can find it, the rhythmic idea has a square around it. The idea appears in the first two measures and then is repeated in measures five and six, and then again in measures nine and ten.

Rhythmic Idea

Remember, a good blues solo doesn't need a lot of notes and it doesn't have to be complicated. Keep it simple. After you've played these solos, try building your own solos over the 12-bar blues progression using the suggestions from this section of the book.

Fingerpicking Blues Solos

This section contains fingerpicking blues solos. These solos are written in two different styles: those which have a *steady bass* and those which have an *alternating bass*. In both of these fingerpicking styles, the right-hand thumb plays the bass strings (6, 5, and 4) and the right-hand fingers (usually 1 or 2) play the melody (strings 1, 2, and 3). **Generally, the notes written with the stems going down are played with the thumb, and the notes with the stems going up are played with the right-hand fingers (usually the first or second finger).**

In the *steady bass* style, the thumb plays the same bass note on each beat of the measure. This note has the same letter name as the chord name for that measure. The fingers play with the thumb or in between the thumb strokes. The choice of which finger to use is up to you. This style of soloing was commonly used by early blues guitarists. If you do not know the meaning of a particular notation, refer to the section on "How To Read The Music" at the beginning of this book.

The next solo is a fingerpicking solo in the key of E using the steady bass style.

This blues solo is in the key of A and also uses the steady bass style.

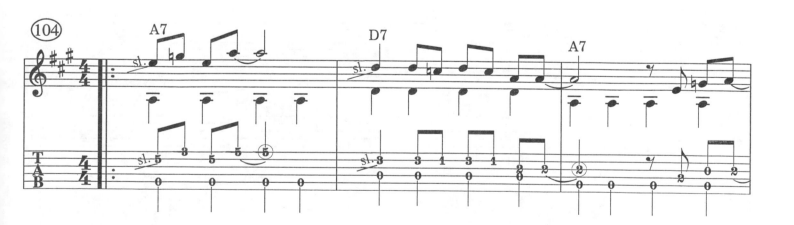

Strum with the right-hand
first finger.

Another type of fingerpicking blues solo is called *alternating bass*. In this style, the thumb alternates between two different notes on each beat of the measure. The fingers play the melody. **In the alternating bass style, while playing the notes in each measure, try to hold the chord which is written above the measure.** The chord may have to be modified slightly by lifting off a finger, or adding a finger to play the written notes. Hold as much of the chord as possible.

The next fingerpicking solo uses the alternating bass style.

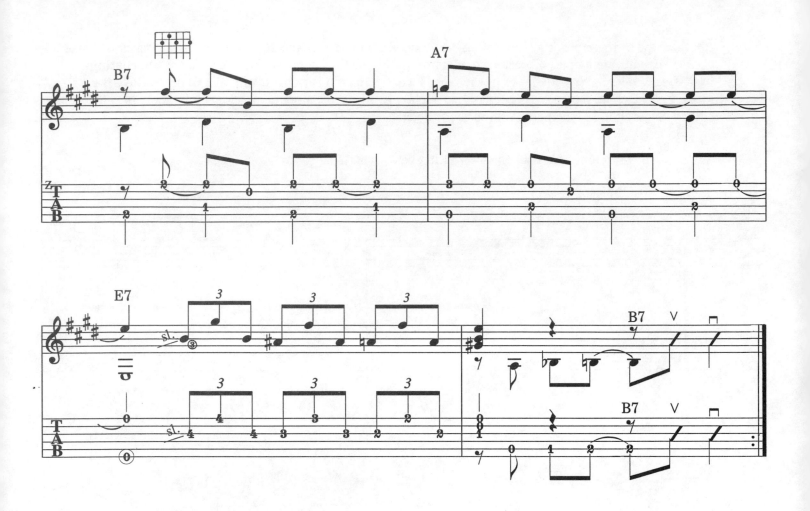

Try creating your own fingerpicking blues solos using the steady bass and alternating bass techniques. Use the blues scale to make up the melody.